T0286199

POCKET STUDY SKILLS

*Series Editor: **Kate Williams**, Oxford Brookes University, UK*
Illustrations by Sallie Godwin

For the time-pushed student, the *Pocket Study Skills* pack a lot of advice into a little book. Each guide focuses on a single crucial aspect of study, giving you step-by-step guidance, handy tips and clear advice on how to approach the important areas which will continually be at the core of your studies.

Published
14 Days to Exam Success
Blogs, Wikis, Podcasts and More
Brilliant Writing Tips for Students
Completing Your PhD
Doing Research
Getting Critical
Planning Your Essay
Planning Your PhD
Reading and Making Notes
Referencing and Understanding Plagiarism
Science Study Skills
Success in Groupwork
Time Management
Writing for University

Further titles in preparation

Pocket Study Skills
Series Standing Order
ISBN 978-0230-21605-1
(outside North America only)

You can receive future titles in this series as they are published by placing a standing order. Please contact your bookseller or, in case of difficulty, write to us at the address below with your name and address, the title of the series and the ISBN quoted above.

Customer Services Department,
Macmillan Distribution Ltd
Houndmills, Basingstoke, Hampshire
RG21 6XS England

POCKET STUDY SKILLS

Kate Williams

Emily Bethell Judith Lawton Clare Parfitt-Brown
Mary Richardson Victoria Rowe

COMPLETING YOUR YOUR PHD

First published 2011 by
PALGRAVE MACMILLAN

Red Globe Press in the UK is an imprint of Macmillan Education Limited, registered in England, company number 01755588, of 4 Crinan Street, London, N1 9XW

Red Globe Press is the global academic imprint of the above companies and has companies and representatives throughout the world.

Red Globe Press® is a registered trademark in the United States, the United Kingdom, Europe and other countries

ISBN-13: 978-0-230-29281-9

This book is printed on paper suitable for recycling and made from fully managed and sustained forest sources. Logging, pulping and manufacturing processes are expected to conform to the environmental regulations of the country of origin.

A catalogue record for this book is available from the British Library.

A catalog record for this book is available from the Library of Congress.

10 9 8 7 6 5 4 3 2 1
20 19 18 17 16 15 14 13 12 11

Contents

About the authors

This book is written by the same group of authors as *Planning Your PhD*.

Kate Williams manages Upgrade, the Study Advice Service at Oxford Brookes University, UK. She has worked with students from Foundation to PhD level and has written a range of books and materials on study skills. She is the Pocket Study Skills series editor.

Emily Bethell completed her interdisciplinary PhD in Biology, Anthropology and Psychology in 2009 and now works as a Senior Lecturer in Primatology and Animal Behaviour at Liverpool John Moores University, UK.

Judith Lawton is an EAL consultant and former Deputy Head of Hounslow Language Service. She has 40 years teaching and teacher training experience and completed her doctoral research in bilingual learner education.

Clare Parfitt-Brown is a Senior Lecturer in Dance at the University of Chichester, UK. Her PhD focused on the history of the cancan and led to ongoing research into the cultural histories of popular dance practices.

Mary Richardson completed an ESRC-funded PhD investigating the assessment of Citizenship Education in 2008. She is now a Senior Lecturer in Education at Froebel College, Roehampton University, UK and continues to develop research in the areas of assessment and citizenship education.

Victoria Rowe worked as a piano teacher for many years prior to completing her PhD in 2008. She is currently a Teaching Associate at the University of Sheffield, UK and also works as a freelance researcher.

Acknowledgements

Many people have contributed to this book and we would like to thank them all. The insights and experiences of many research students form the bedrock of the book: those who have attended Kate's workshops over the years at the University of Oxford, Oxford Brookes University, and most of all Roehampton University, are now joined by participants in workshops run by other co-authors in their universities.

Thanks too to the workshop participants, critical readers and anonymous reviewers who will see their observations and comments directly reflected in the text. Particular thanks to:

Mike Castelli, Principal Lecturer in Education, Roehampton University, UK and PhD student (by publication)
Gordon Clark (FBA), Halford Mackinder Professor of Geography, University of Oxford, UK, who is always generous with his insights and thought provoking in his comments
Dr Barbara Crossouard, Director of EdD programme, University of Sussex, UK
Professor David Evans, Head of Department of Life Sciences, Oxford Brookes University, UK
Dr Dianne Gereluk, University of Calgary, Canada

Andrew Harker, Brunel University, UK, PhD student

Dr Kate Hone, Department of Information Systems and Computing and Director of Graduate School, Brunel University, UK

Liverpool Hope University PhD Group: Stephen Axon, Alyson Blanchard, Sasha Deepwell, Aisha Ijaz, Marc Wells

Dr Stephanie Pitts, Senior Lecturer in Music, University of Sheffield, UK

Sarah Rubidge, Professor of Choreography and New Media, University of Chichester, UK

Thanks to Sallie Godwin for capturing so much more than words can do in her astute illustrations. And finally, thanks to the brilliant team at Palgrave Macmillan, endlessly supportive and creative in finding solutions at every point.

Introduction

Completing Your PhD is about just that. We all completed our PhDs, and took between 4 and 7 years to do so. This is a huge chunk of life, and after the first flush of energy in starting a PhD (the subject of *Planning Your PhD* in this series), you move into a different mode. The whole journey towards the PhD is a series of 'moves'. When you know the moves, you can play the game, carry off the performance. You have to sustain your purpose and identity as a researcher and move towards the specific end point of achieving your doctorate.

Achieving a PhD is a bumpy road. All sorts of pressures can pull you away and prevent you from maintaining your focus: families grow and change around you, work becomes pressing, funding runs out. We achieved our PhDs by many routes – full time, part time, a mix, some funded time, some not, working, not working. Some people do not make it: in the UK, 75% full time PhD students and 35% part time complete within 7 years (HEFCE 2007). Put another way, 25% of full time students and an awesome 65% part time do not complete within the statistics-gathering time frame. This is not to suggest that time spent researching (but not getting a doctorate) is necessarily wasted, and part time students in particular undertake research for a huge variety of reasons. Nevertheless, this figure must represent considerable individual disappointment, frustration and opportunities lost.

We wrote this book because we thought we had something to say about the process of sustaining the PhD to completion. It is not all about the loneliness of the long-distance researcher. You belong to a research community – most likely, several – and key to sustaining research over a period of time is to find these communities, develop your networks and contacts, and to join them!

Talking about your research is fundamental to developing your ideas (and staying sane!). Talking is also an essential channel by which you communicate with your research community, in one-to-one discussion, informal seminars and workshops. Where an oral examination is part of the examination process of the doctorate, the habit of talking is essential preparation. In Part 4 we consider the arenas in which you develop your talking skills, and in Part 5 we consider how you draw on all these skills in your viva.

Writing is the other channel by which you communicate your research. This too takes a whole range of forms – progress statements, papers, articles – which help you build skills, a track record and stamina for the final submission in which you draw together all your research in a particular format. In Part 2 we consider the forms of writing you use to develop and communicate your ideas. In Part 3 we consider the writing involved in the thesis.

What's in a name?
'Thesis' or 'Dissertation' –
it's still a PhD!

Doing a PhD is a great way to develop contacts around the world. We have stayed in touch with fellow PhD students around the globe and we are developing our own networks worldwide through our disciplines. In the essential aspects, we have learnt that the experience of PhD students around the world is a shared one, despite superficial differences. We hope this book will have something to say to PhD students wherever you are …

Our companion book, *Planning Your PhD*, starts at the point where you may be considering doing a PhD, through becoming a researcher to some of the key pieces of writing you will do in your first year of research. *Completing Your PhD* starts from where *Planning Your PhD* left off.

This is how we planned the book

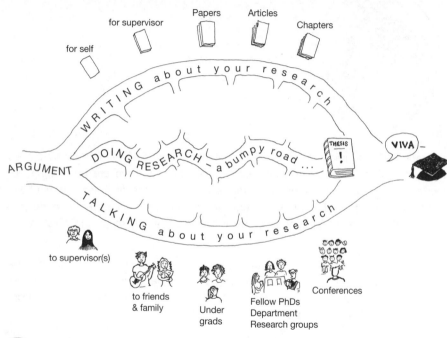

for self

for supervisor

Papers

Articles

Chapters

WRITING about your research

ARGUMENT

DOING RESEARCH – a bumpy road ...

THESIS !

VIVA –

TALKING about your research

to supervisor(s)

to friends & family

Under grads

Fellow PhDs Department Research groups

Conferences

About *Completing Your PhD*

Part 1 The road to completion gives an overview of what is involved in completing your PhD.

Part 2 Writing and publication considers why you write, who you write for and how to write for publication as you work towards your PhD.

Part 3 Writing your thesis considers the thesis – whatever form it takes – as an examination document, and how to organise and structure it.

Part 4 Talking and presenting focuses on some of the ways in which you talk about your research, and how to present your work to expert audiences at academic conferences.

Part 5 The oral examination: the viva offers practical advice about how to prepare and how to perform at the oral examination, the second strand of the final exam in many parts of the world.

Part 6 Life after your PhD takes a look at the PhD as the beginning of the next phase of life.

This section provides an overview of what lies ahead in your PhD journey, from roughly the mid-point to your destination: when you submit your thesis, and, where there is an oral examination, the opportunity to defend your thesis in the viva.

Every researcher's journey is unique. There is, nevertheless, a common core to the shape of a research project – something like this:

The first loop of the process – the literature review, or context for practice in practice-based PhDs – is the powerhouse for the PhD. You are getting to grips with what's out there, what is already known, how this is conceptualised and the different approaches used in related research. All the time you will be refining and refocusing your research question, until it sits in the gap in knowledge, is the right size, is researchable.

The second loop is your methodology, which is likely to dominate the middle phase of your PhD. You will find you focus much more on the methodologies of the material you read, and use what you notice to refine your own. Just as you critique other people's methods, others will critique yours – so you want it to stand up to scrutiny.

The third loop is putting it all together: what you have established, how it relates to the body of knowledge out there, and the contribution you have made to the field. This is the communication loop. You have something to say, and have to make sense of it and

The research process

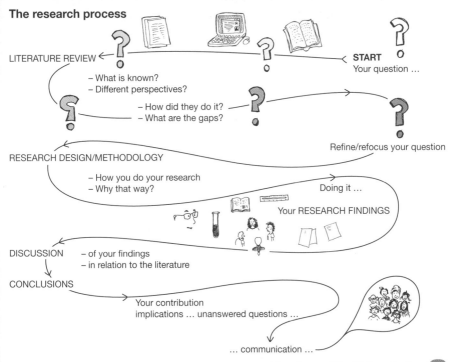

LITERATURE REVIEW ←

START
Your question …

– What is known?
– Different perspectives?

– How did they do it?
– What are the gaps?

Refine/refocus your question

RESEARCH DESIGN/METHODOLOGY

– How you do your research
– Why that way?

Doing it …

Your RESEARCH FINDINGS

DISCUSSION – of your findings
– in relation to the literature

CONCLUSIONS

Your contribution
implications … unanswered questions …

… communication …

The shape of the PhD project 3

communicate it, writing and talking about it. By communicating you take your place in the academic community.

All this has to happen within time limits. You may have set a limit on the time *you* want to devote to the PhD project. Funding bodies certainly set limits. Your institution will be looking to their completion targets. So time is a big player from the mid-point of your PhD onwards.

PhD by publication can be more flexible for those who cannot undertake a full time PhD, but there is always the balance between having enough time for research and writing and taking too long ...

2 Managing the PhD

A PhD is a big project to undertake, and to achieve it you need to put time and energy into managing it. At any given point you need to have a plan to manage your:

▶ time
▶ tasks, great and small
▶ resources.

Managing your time

There are no magic ways of managing time other than finding strategies that work for you. Here are some suggestions.

Your road map

First, see the bigger picture, the whole process to the finish. You know where you are now. You know the date when you have to submit your thesis, and roughly when your viva will be.

Workshop 1: The road to completion

Try to visualise your pathway from where you are NOW (don't look back and include what you've done up to now) to when you complete your doctorate – submitting your thesis and viva examination.

→ Take a large sheet of paper – A3 is ideal
→ Put yourself at the bottom: **start**
→ Show your completion points at the top: **submitting your thesis** and **viva**
→ Sketch the journey in between
→ Show trouble spots
→ Mark in milestones – including publications, especially if you are doing your PhD by the publication route
→ Mark out the time phases and deadlines

Give yourself 15 minutes.

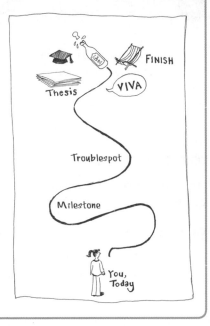

This road map will help you see what you need to do to achieve the body of work that will make up your PhD. Once you can see the component parts – whether it is your publications, developing practice or chapters in the traditional 'big book' thesis – it will feel less like a giant octopus and more like a sequence of phases or set of building blocks you can create and control.

Timelines and deadlines

Now take a closer look at the lead-in to your next milestone, and plan your time and tasks in more detail. Work back from the deadline you have given yourself and log what you have to do to get there. Deadlines are helpful when you are working on the component parts of your research, but less productive when you are looking at longer time periods.

To love your deadlines, they must be realistic, so you can achieve them. If you find they are unrealistic and make you miserable, adjust your plan accordingly.

Chapters are convenient blocks to drive your time planning:

- Work **back** from when you want to complete a chapter. Mark in all the things you need to do – and when – to get there.
- Then check that you are not being overambitious – work forwards, then back again.

When it feels right, you have a plan …

I've noticed that people tend to overestimate what they can achieve in nearer deadlines (weeks or months), and underestimate what can be achieved in longer deadlines – like years!

I love deadlines. I love the whooshing sound they make as they fly by.

Douglas Adams
(circa 1979 in Simpson 2003 p236)

Here's an example:

	Weeks/dates						
Method chapter: Tasks/phases							
Finalise access and ethical permission	▪ ▪ ▪						
Conduct pilot study/project	▪ ▪ ▪						
Preliminary analysis. Collect feedback from participants		▪ ▪ ▪ ▪					
Write up pilot study		▬▬▬					
Adjust method if necessary			▪ ▪ ▪				
Write up method for main study or project, including any adjustments			▬▬▬▬▬				
Conduct main study				▪ ▪ ▪ ▪ ▪ ▪ ▪			
Analyse results					▪ ▪ ▪ ▪ ▪ ▪ ▪		
Write up analysis and results sections						▬▬▬▬▬	

Doing/thinking/planning: ▪ ▪ ▪ ▪   Writing: ▬▬▬

In this example of the work involved in a Method chapter, you can see how thinking and doing lead to specific sections of writing. But no diagram can quite capture the iterative nature of research: backwards and forwards, onwards and upwards …

The research spiral

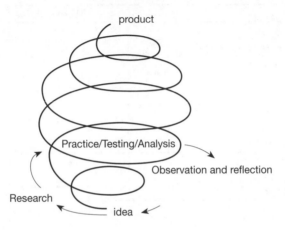

A simple hand-drawn line is just as good as a diagram, and can extend over as many pages as you need. Use any kind of timeline you like – what matters is that you have one.

If you keep these plans up to date, you will have an ongoing map of your research plan – useful in discussion with your supervisor(s).

Managing tasks

Here are some of the strategies and habits we have developed:

▶ Decide when you will work on your PhD and when you will not. For part time PhD students this may in part be dictated by your working hours.

▶ Having too much time may be more difficult to manage than having too little! As a part time student you will get those breaks from study and come back refreshed.

▶ Know when you work best on the hard stuff – early bird or night owl?

▶ Work out what you do when: for example, check emails at low energy times (after lunch? evenings?) so you can go straight into work at your most productive times.

▶ Watch out for your favourite ways of frittering away precious research time. Checking emails, online activities, departmental activity, cups of tea, cooking, cleaning … are not research!

▶ Do little and often – it helps you keep in touch with your thoughts and reduces your start-up time. Think about start-up slots, working slots, review slots, housekeeping slots.

▶ Work out what you can do in little bits of time, and what you need a big chunk of time for – there aren't many of these, especially for part timers.

▶ Write a TO DO list every day. Include big and small items, research and other activities, and give yourself

I prioritise my list as I go – and keep a bin for things that are not important, and not urgent!

the satisfaction of ticking them off. Watch out for any item you carry over 3 days. Is it too big to do in a day? Do you feel stressed about it? Break it

down into smaller chunks and take the first step today. Just look at it.

▶ Reward yourself when you complete something tricky: a cup of tea or a walk round the block – incentives do work.

▶ Take a full 2-day break from the project (at least occasionally). A good weekend break can work wonders for your productivity.

Managing resources

There are two aspects to this: resources for your research and resources for you.

Resources for your research

Look at the weeks and months ahead in your timeline. What do you need for this to happen? Access to libraries? Labs? Equipment? People? Participants? Lead-in time is probably about twice as long as you think. To avoid delays start organising well in advance. Take into account your personal circumstances – visa rejections and delays are notorious for delaying research by months!

If you use shared resources such as laboratory space, or expensive and scarce equipment, you need to consider others' needs too. People working on shorter time scales (such as Masters students) will often be granted priority of access to these, as well as your supervisors' time and attention.

If you require participants for Psychological studies then early in the academic year you may well find lots of keen students actively searching for experiments to take part in to raise money, or gain participant credits (in Psychology departments for example). Summer holidays, on the other hand, will be dead – you don't want to be looking for participants then!

Resources for you

Top of this list is ongoing finance. Paid employment is the essential source of finance for most research students, and can be a source of frustration in competing for your time. It can also be positive – helpful in defining the time you have available to spend on your research, and in keeping you grounded

I've found that inspiration for a new way forward or the resolution to a particular problem comes to me while I'm not actively 'researching'. Having time away gives you some distance on the project ...

and sane. Where your research is related to your professional practice, both can be enriched by the insights and reflection you bring from one to the other.

It can be frustrating to have to take time out of your research to make applications for finance (great and small). So build in time to spend on these essential aspects of life right from the start, and include them in your overall timeline as well as your weekly timetable.

Managing 'time off' is as essential as managing 'time on'. Give yourself time to eat well, exercise, enjoy social time with friends and family. Holidays may end up bottom of your To Do list (if they appear at all). Book holiday time in advance, spend it away from the office/email, and do not take work with you!

3 Looking ahead to completion

It is worth pausing for a moment to look ahead to the finish, to allow the format of your final submission to influence what you do now.

In all countries you submit a written document, which will dominate your thoughts and planning and take up your time. If your PhD includes a substantial practice element, this too will absorb your time and focus. In those countries that include a viva in the final examination, you have a great additional opportunity to 'defend' your thesis in face-to-face discussion with experts in your field.

The questions examiners ask in an oral examination are those that any fellow specialist in your field will want to know about your research (and quite a few non-specialists too). There is nothing mysterious about the questions – these are the questions your readers will be asking as they read. It's the answers you need to work on!

Workshop 2: Questions everyone wants to know about your research (especially your examiners!)

Take a notebook or pad of Post-it® notes and jot down the answers to these questions.

1 **What's it about?**
   Why are you carrying out the research? What is your purpose?

2 **What is your methodology?**
   Why did you design it that way?

3 **What is the bigger picture?**
   What are the likely implications of your research? How might it make a difference?

These questions point you to the fundamentals of your research that you need to focus on throughout and will be addressing whenever you talk and write about your research – with your supervisory team, at presentations and conferences.

This is what it's all about, surely? Why else would you spend 3+ years of your life working to place a small brick into the gap in knowledge you identified? Think back to what motivated you to undertake this research. It will drive you through justifying your research, to the eventual contribution you make.

From an extrinsic point of view, your contribution also represents the 'value' of your research to the research community and other interested parties or stakeholders. So how do you make this contribution?

First and foremost, you make your **contribution to scholarship, to a body of knowledge**, and you disseminate this through publication, the 'literature'. Scholarship evidenced in writing is the channel of communication with other researchers, who will in turn cite your work as evidence for a statement or argument they are seeking to make. You are adding one little piece to the jigsaw of knowledge. This is the means by which your research enters the mainstream and by which you make a difference.

This idea can take a bit of getting used to, especially for researchers who are driven by the desire to make a tangible difference – to a process, to a community, to an injustice, to policy, to practice – and particularly relevant to those taking professional doctorates.

If you can see **implications for policy** or **practice**, you can also outline them in your conclusions. You might be lucky enough to return to a work situation where you can implement some of your findings (again, particularly if you are doing a professional doctorate), but it is more likely that you will have to leave it to others to pick up and use. Your PhD is not a recipe for change, but an argument for knowledge and better or different understanding with *implications* for policy or practice.

Finally, you might find yourself turning over in your mind all the research questions you wish you could pursue. Make a note of these as you go: it may help you to identify an important limitation to your research. You will be able to identify these as **implications for future research** when you set them out in your conclusions.

WRITING AND PUBLICATION

Part 2 is about writing: why you write, who you write for, and how you write for publication on the PhD journey. The thesis itself is the subject of Part 3.

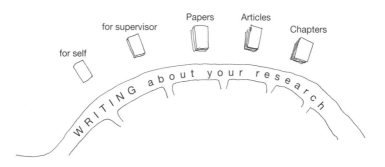

Write for yourself

A lot of what you write will be read by no one but yourself.

Booth, Columb and Williams (1995) propose three reasons for researchers to write for themselves:

- write to remember
- write to understand
- write to gain perspective (pp. 8–9).

Since we (the authors) spent many a session discussing these three reasons, we took these headings as the starting point for considering the writing you do as a researcher.

To these three reasons, we add a fourth:

- Write to get better at it.

Write to remember

A PhD involves a series of decisions and developments in thought that occur over many years (at least 3, and often more). You will certainly not remember all you read 3 years ago but it will have influenced your thought processes.

Your note taking will evolve throughout the PhD and the
filing system you have at the end may be very different
from the system you started off with. This is fine – it
is called learning and that is the point of a PhD.

Some suggestions

- Use a **separate
  notebook** for the
  different sections
  or chapters of
  the PhD.
- Remind yourself
  **why you didn't   START   FINISH
  do something**
  as well as why you did. It could help you to anticipate awkward methodological
  questions in the viva (see Workshop 2).
- **Keep your old diaries**: to track when you met people, had discussions, meetings,
  attended or presented at conferences, to substantiate those vague memories/
  ideas …
- Always **include references** with your notes – a great time saver later on.

- Compile a **single set of references (**or **'bibliography')** from the beginning, so that it grows with each chapter, taking the stress out of the gigantic task of compiling it at the end.
- Note where you can **access different sources**: keep folders of PDFs; links in bibliographic software; notes of libraries and databases you used – all useful when you revisit them, which you will.
- Make a list of the **major names** in your field, their expertise and affiliations (which universities they are at). This will help you to become familiar with the academic social group of which you will ultimately become a member.

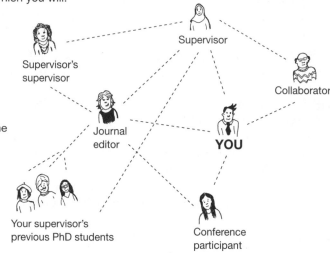

Write to understand

Writing about what you have read will help you to organise your thoughts and to understand the logic, methods and findings of others. Putting your own ideas onto paper will help you to articulate your own line of thought. This will highlight any grey areas in your argument and any unwise assumptions.

Write down, not up! Writing up sounds like something you do sometime later. Write it down now, while it's fresh in your mind and you can see it out there.

If you find yourself struggling to understand what someone else has written, have a go at capturing the key points in your own words and discuss it with your supervisor.

Write to gain perspective

Booth et al. (1995) are of the view that when we get our thoughts onto paper, we see them in a 'clearer light, one that is always brighter and less flattering' (p. 9).

Everyone who writes anything will have experienced the excitement and elation of getting going, getting something down … so yes, write it. Then leave it and come back to it in the cold light of day, and …

... the editor in you will take over, and it may look less good. But don't be too harsh – make changes, leave it and come back again later. What you have written could well be better than you thought ...

As you become a writer, you move between reading, thinking, writing and editing. Don't attempt these last two at the same time, or you will never get anything written!

Write to get better at it

Doing a PhD is like learning a new language. You will learn new words, new concepts and new ways of communicating these.

Different subject areas favour different styles of writing, ranging along a continuum from the more objective to the more reflective and interpretational.

Science ... Technology ... Social sciences ... Humanities ... Arts
More objective ... ... More reflective/interpretational

As you enter the academic community of your discipline, you may need to make a conscious effort to develop an appropriate writing style. You need to talk the talk, in order for your work to 'sit' comfortably in the field.

But try to square it with George Orwell's advice: 'Never use a long word when a short one will do' (1946).

Words that help argument

Be aware of how writers make choices in the language they use to show how they position themselves in relation to the research they are commenting on:

Smith (2003)	points out argues maintains claims concludes suggests	that	preventative medicine is far more cost effective, and therefore better adapted to the developing world.

University of Manchester (2010)

Careful choice of verbs can signal doubt ('claims'), hesitancy ('suggests'), specific interest ('points out') and so on. This is a fundamental skill in conveying your argument and will ensure that you are never merely descriptive.

Workshop 3: How do they do it?

Look at how your academic peers write.

→ Take a close look at a couple of pages in peer-reviewed articles in your subject. List the words and phrases the authors use to introduce their comments about other writers.

→ And try them out in your writing!

No doubt you will come across examples of poor writing. Look suspiciously at anything that seems overcomplicated, and if it could be expressed more clearly or more simply it is probably not a good model for you. You will develop your own voice, and your own style of writing – do so with confidence.

6 Writing for others

I didn't feel qualified to write for learned journals to begin with, but I did contribute to the monthly magazine of my professional body.

It was quite easy to imagine that I was writing this work for my friends to read, and to shape and phrase it accordingly.

It is not easy to preserve the right combination of both humility (they are real human beings who likely know much more than me) and courage (they may be wrong and I need to be brave enough to raise that possibility).

It helps you to write well when you know who you are writing for. Not having a particular reader in mind makes it harder to write. Fix your actual reader clearly in your mind, and write for them. If you are writing for a wider audience, create a kalei-doscope of potential readers in your mind (pick out a few individuals from a room of conference participants, practitioners, fellow researchers), and imagine each one reading what you are writing. Don't assume that they know the subject area in the way you do – you need to make explicit the premises or assumptions on which you base your work. Now write!

Writing to inform and convince others

Your supervisory team will be your first and most consistent critical readers. If you can write in a way that explains your ideas clearly to them, and convince them of the worth of your argument, then you are on the right track.

Throughout your PhD you will need to convince different people of the validity of your line of inquiry or reasoning – in your upgrade to PhD, and ethics and progress reports for example (see *Planning Your PhD*). If you can find out who these individuals are, you can work out where you need to pitch your writing. More generalist academic audiences will require less technical jargon and a clearer rationale and justification of methods.

Workshop 4: Explaining your research

In one sentence, summarise your research to three different audiences:

researchers in your discipline (such as your supervisory team)	
academics in a non-related discipline (such as other faculty members)	
family or friends	

Using feedback

Publication brought me some useful feedback from the field and some encouraging signs that my work was on the right lines.

Academic writing involves a huge amount of redrafting, editing and refining following feedback.

The acknowledgements in any published paper or book will give you an insight into the feedback the authors gained from contributing individuals, editors and reviewers. Getting feedback is part of the process; the question is how you use it.

You may choose to accept feedback – 'constructive criticism' – or argue against it, but either way you will learn from it. Comments on one section of your writing could equally well apply to another – it's up to you to carry your learning with you, not just make 'corrections'. Comments from your supervisor(s) may sound critical and rather harsh, but they are usually made with good reason, and you should become a better writer for it.

Supervisors may disagree among themselves. You can use disagreements between supervisors to refine your own argument – they have presented you with the counter-arguments to your case. Learning to anticipate criticisms and to build this into your text will make your own argument stronger. It is good preparation for the viva.

> *My supervisor always told me that I write to understand in the first draft, and then, after incorporating her (often extensive) comments, write to communicate in the later drafts.*

There will also be feedback which, from time to time, feels obstructive to the progress of your research. Feedback on ethics applications can be one of the toughest forms of feedback to handle. If you do not pass the ethics panel you cannot start your research, but this suggests that there are ethical implications to your research that you have not fully considered or have not fully justified. You will need to act on it.

7 Writing to publish

Publication is the primary means by which your research becomes known in the field: it is how you make your contribution to 'the literature'. Because of this, publication has become the proxy by which you and your work are judged for a whole range of purposes, the narrow neck of the bottle to academic success.

Publication is highly instrumental. Aside from your genuine desire to share your findings with others, publication is a core measure of academic success. Publication in peer-reviewed journals will determine your standing in the Research Excellence Framework (REF) in the UK, and equivalent systems in other countries. From here it influences your 'value' to your institution and future employers.

I found it important to my post-PhD career that I published during my PhD. In the current research climate universities are concerned with output ...

Publication before your viva not only helps you develop your argument, but it also offers an external benchmark that demonstrates your ability as a researcher. If you are working towards your PhD by the publication route, publication in peer-reviewed journals is, quite simply, a must.

So ... no pressure then!

I started writing journal articles after I'd completed the PhD – I'm on my third now – I wish I'd started earlier!

The response to published articles helps the author to reflect upon the quality of her/ his current research, its focus, direction and contribution to the professional discourse, and in doing so to refine the focus of research.

Consider the impact measurements

Writing for publication is time consuming, so target your journals strategically. In science and the social sciences (less so in the arts) journals are given an Impact Factor (IF) according to how widely cited articles in those journals are. Journals with a high IF are widely read and highly cited. But do read between the lines when considering IFs. Specialist journals will often have a low IF because they have a small, targeted audience. However, the true impact may be high precisely because your message will reach the most important people in your field.

Once published, the value of your research can be assessed by the wider academic community. An indicator of this is the citation rate – the number of times your work is cited by others as evidence for points or arguments they want to make. This will provide you, as an academic, with an 'H number' which reflects not only how many papers you have published, but how often you have been cited in other publications. The H index (Hirsch Index) allows academics to assess not only another academic's output (n) of papers, but also their impact (h). As with the IF, if used wisely, this measure can help to provide an indicator of output and quality.

Into print

To conclude Part 2 we revisit headings of the 'Hints for publication' outlined in *Planning Your PhD* (pp. 113–15), and add some detail to how you might use them to help you plan your publication strategy.

In some disciplines, journals are not the only option for publication. Networking may lead to invitations to contribute a chapter to a book or edited collection. These also carry academic esteem.

Hint 1: Get familiar with the journals

Peer-reviewed journals publish articles written and vetted by experts in the field.

The impact factor will have some bearing on the likelihood of acceptance – so pick your journal carefully. Consult your supervisor early on about familiarising yourself with journals in your field.

Look at the range of forms that articles take:

- data-based papers
- reviews
- case studies
- shorter papers – like 'Brief Communications' or 'Letters'
- articles in special guest-edited issues on a specialised topic
- research in progress.

Hint 2: Think ahead

The conventional publication process usually takes at least 9 months from submission. Since publication will tend to be concentrated in the later phases of your PhD, you will need to look carefully at your publication plans in the time ahead. Free access online journals (for example, the Public Library of Science series, PLoS) have much shorter publication times, and could be worth considering if you want to publish before you complete your PhD.

Hint 3: Find out the authorship conventions for doctoral students in your discipline

Agree the authorship of papers early on: joint or single authorship? Order of authors? These can be contentious issues, and you need to discuss them with your supervisor. Everyone needs to be clear about the expectations from the beginning – more of an issue in science-based subjects than in the arts.

For students doing a PhD by publication, the issue of authorship is key: you must be able to claim majority rights to any co-authored work, and support this in writing. Hopefully your colleagues will support you by placing your name first as the lead author on this occasion.

Hint 4: Match your paper to the models in the journal you are submitting to

Scrutinise the format, style, referencing and instructions to authors – and follow the guidelines to the letter. The Editor will decide whether to send your submission for review. Typically the reviewers will read your work and report back to the Editor suggesting 'Accept', 'Reject' or 'Resubmit with revisions'.

You may find that the journals you read are the ones you want to publish in – and that you have developed a good intuitive sense of the style they require.

Hint 5: Draft and redraft

Your first draft will not be good enough.

Draft 2 will be better. You will have matched it to the model.

Draft 3 will be better still. You'll have worked on your language and expression. Show it to some colleagues and ask for their comments.

Draft 4 should be looking good … ready to submit?

Hint 6: Ask the editor for *advice*

At draft 3 or 4 (when you have acted on feedback and checked with your supervisor), consider sending it to the editor *not* as a submission but to ask: *Do you have any advice?* Ask if you can send an abstract: *Is the abstract suitable for your journal?* Find out too about timescales for publication (3–6 months? 2 years?). This will have implications for the currency of your research as well as your life plans.

But don't use the editor as a screening process for correcting things you should have corrected already. Rejection is the immediate price you will pay, and you may also risk immediate rejection of a future submission.

Hint 7: Don't pick a fight

Academic debates in any field tend to be polarised. Don't pick a side, but show the thread you are pursuing. Use moderate and reasoned language. In a peer-reviewed journal your paper will be sent to specialists in precisely your field. They may turn out to be the gatekeepers to your future career.

Hint 8: Rejection? Don't lose heart

It happens to everyone! The best journals have rejection rates of about 70%–90%. Take constructive criticism on board, make changes and send it to another journal. Don't send it to another journal without making the changes. They are likely to be using the same relatively small pool of reviewers.

The final audience for your writing is your PhD examiners. These very special readers require your writing to be in a very particular form – the subject of Part 3.

WRITING YOUR THESIS

Part 3 is about writing the thesis, whether it takes the form of a collection of papers, the 'big book' or something in between. Whatever form yours takes, your PhD thesis will be a truly extraordinary document. It is probably the biggest document you have ever written, to be read by the smallest audience: your examiners.

The focus of Part 3 therefore is exclusively on the thesis, the biggest examination document of them all.

Yes, your thesis is first and foremost an exam document. Your preparation of the thesis needs to be geared to meeting – hopefully exceeding – the expectations of your examiner. So …

Start thinking about your examiner

Who will examine your thesis?
- ☐ Internal examiner?
- ☐ External examiner?
- ☐ A committee?
  How many people?
  Who are they?

If the assessment system in the country you are studying in includes external examiner(s), think about who might be suitable. If the system involves an exam committee of internal academics, you have more opportunity to get to know something about them – for better or worse. Either way, seeing potential examiners as real live people with their own outlook and perspectives gives you real readers to write for.

You are never permitted to select your own examiner, but you will be expected to have some suggestions, however vague to start with. Your supervisor(s) will let you know if your suggestions are realistic.

Considerations:

- A high-profile academic may need to be booked a long time ahead. Will your university pay their travel expenses, especially if they are coming from abroad? If not, will they be coming to your country for a conference …? If you have to wait for your viva, are you OK about this? Might the delay impact on your funding?
- An examiner new to the role may have enthusiasm, more time, fewer preconceptions but equally could be 'overzealous', wanting to prove themselves – possibly at your expense.

- You would be wise to suggest an examiner with whom you are in accord in some way: stylistically, methodologically or philosophically. If different members of an exam committee have very different approaches (rivalries even), how might it affect their examination of your work?

The examiners' checklist

Examiners follow guidelines laid down by the awarding institution and by independent regulatory bodies. In the UK, the Quality Assurance Agency (QAA, 2004) provides guidelines for examiners and states that 'outcomes should relate to the student's ability to conceptualise, design and implement a research study, ultimately producing a piece of work that will inform the subject and/or professional practice'.

The examiners will have a checklist of points on which they must base their 'Preliminary report' on the thesis, something like this:

The type of questions the examiner has to report on	
1	Does the thesis demonstrate acknowledgement of appropriate sources and related material?
2	Does the thesis represent an original contribution to knowledge of the subject by the discovery of new facts, methodology or theory?
3	Does the thesis represent an original contribution to knowledge of the subject by the exercise of independent critical powers?
4	Is the thesis satisfactory as regards literary presentation and succinctness?
5	Is the abstract of the thesis satisfactory?
6	In the case of a candidate whose research programme is part of a collaborative group project, does the thesis indicate clearly the individual contribution and the extent of the collaboration?

Reproduced (with minor alterations) with thanks to Oxford Brookes
University Research degrees subcommittee (2010).

A checklist like this concentrates the mind on the fact that your examiners will be looking for certain characteristics and qualities, and your task is to ensure they will find them.

Practicalities 1

Check: how long will your thesis be?

Check carefully with your institution to be absolutely clear about the essentials. Here are some typical lengths, but there is a much wider range:

PhD/DPhil: 60,000–100,000 words

Professional doctorate: 40,000–60,000

Practice-based doctorate: 40,000–50,000

PhD by publication: The overall length of the portfolio of work may be comparable to a traditional PhD. However, individual publications will vary in length, so institutions may not set a word limit. The common element is a critical/reflective supporting statement, typically 20,000–30,000 words, offering a rationale for why the body of work should be considered as a serious contribution to research.

Are the bibliography/references and appendices included in your word count?

(Sometimes they are, sometimes they aren't!)

Practicalities 2

Working methods – some suggestions

▶ **Create a template** that incorporates all the formatting requirements (margins, font size, headings) and use it for all your chapters from the beginning (see your Handbook). If you apply them at the end it will cause monumental changes throughout your documents, causing you delay – days, if not weeks, of reformatting.

▶ Find out which **referencing software** your department/supervisors/fellow students use. Take advantage of any free training and start using it sooner rather than later.

▶ Collate **appendices** as you go – keep a folder of this information so you can print, photocopy or scan documents easily. This is the additional stuff your examiner may want to see: raw data, images, questionnaires, ethical permissions, interview transcripts.

▶ **Acknowledgements**: keep a list of *everyone* who helped you to conduct your PhD – it never hurts to include names but it may offend to exclude them.

These simple steps will save you weeks of wasted time later on. Trust us; we've been there.

Keep it simple!

The best theses are:

- a confident assertion of the question
- how I did it
- what the results were.

(with thanks to Gordon Clark)

There are, of course, infinite variations on this theme, but it's a good place to start …

Discuss chapter structure with your supervisory team as soon as you start thinking about it. Conventions about chapter structure are there for a reason – they are tried and tested ways of presenting argument and evidence in your field. There is no point in alienating your examiners on the first page.

On the other hand, it is *your* thesis! Find out how flexible these structures are in practice, and look at the range of structures used in related PhDs. Once your external examiner is confirmed, hunt for theses they have supervised or examined. This will tell you a lot about their preferred structures and style.

For ideas … browse through theses in the library collection. Even if in the end your chapter structure looks much the same to the reader as others in your discipline, you will have worked it out for yourself. You may find theses that have chapters titled 'literature review', 'results', 'discussion', and theses that do not include the terms at all. These functions will be there, of course, but the chapters are organised thematically, and the titles reflect this.

The following pages show examples (not models!) of the chapter structure of theses loosely based on our own, from the social sciences, arts/humanities and science. While these may be 'typical', these forms are not 'set' within disciplines – every thesis will have its own structure. We have added comments on the order in which we wrote the various sections, to shed a little light on the complex relationship between the process of research, writing and the eventual product.

Chapter outline 1: Social science (education)

This is a fairly 'standard' format for a social science doctorate. It assumes some empirical basis, data collection, analysis and interpretation of results and a discussion in relation to the literature.

Chapter		
Abstract **Acknowledgements** **Contents**		*VERY LAST* *TENTH* *NINTH*
1	**Introduction** ▶ Aims and the significance of the research, why it matters ▶ Scope and structure of thesis – the 'story'	*Written LAST, after the conclusion. Now you can see your pathway clearly and can guide your reader to what lies ahead!*
2	**The research question(s) and statement of the problem** Mapping the issues surrounding the problem	*The FIRST section I wrote*
3/4	**Literature review** It may be in more than one part or even more than one chapter	*SECOND Start here to 'find' your place in the literatures. Models emerge ... what is missing? Where does your research fit? This thread runs through the WHOLE process – the reading never ends ...*

5	**Methodology** (what you did) *THIRD*
	▶ Choosing methods appropriate to your study and explaining them
	▶ Ethical issues and how you managed them
	▶ How you went about it
	▶ What can't be achieved (limits)
6/7	**Results** *FOURTH*
	Likely to be more than one chapter
	▶ What did you find out? What do the data show?
	▶ How do they relate to your aims?
8	**Discussion/implications** of your findings *FIFTH*
	▶ Returning to the literature
	▶ Restatement of the problem addressed
	▶ What contribution have you made?
9	**Conclusion** *SIXTH Must be joined at*
	▶ What was learnt? Reflections *the hip to the introduction,*
	▶ Implications for: scholarship, practice/policy *so start thinking about the*
	(where relevant) *intro as you write*
	▶ Unanswered questions/future research.

Bibliography/references *SEVENTH*
Appendices: 'Exhibits' on which your evidence or discussion depends *EIGHTH*

Chapter outline 2: Arts (dance)

Thesis structures in the arts vary greatly, with themed content chapters emerging from the subject matter itself. Other subjects in the Arts and Humanities, including theoretical studies and those that do not include an empirical base, may adopt a similar pattern. Whatever the eventual structure, all contain these key elements.

Chapter	
Abstract **Contents**	*SIXTH I wrote the abstract immediately after the introduction* *EIGHTH*
1	**Introduction** *FIFTH The introduction* ▶ Personal and academic rationales for the research *was my LAST chapter* ▶ Contexts ▶ Scope and limits of the thesis ▶ Outline of methods ▶ Hint towards your overall argument?
2	**Literature review and methodology** *FIRST* These may be subsections within one chapter, or separate chapters

3(–7)	**Themed content chapters** A range of 3 to 8 in total. In each chapter, a key theme is	*SECOND Written in the order in which they would finally appear*	*THIRD I redrafted all the content chapters*
	outlined and then discussed in detail, combining critical analysis of the literature with examination of source materials. Each chapter has its own conclusion.		
8	**Conclusion** Drawing together the strands and reflecting upon the experience. What are the outcomes that remain unresolved? Are there new questions? The successes and limitations of your study.	*FOURTH*	
Bibliography		*SEVENTH After the abstract. Generated by Endnote, but needed final formatting at the end*	

Chapter outline 3: Science (primate cognition)

A typical science PhD will contain an introduction which reviews the scientific literature (what we currently know and what we would benefit from knowing in the future). This is followed by a series of empirical chapters (what I did and what I found out) and finishes with conclusions (making explicit the importance, or potential impact, of the findings).

Chapter	
Abstract **Acknowledgements** **Contents: lists of appendices, tables and figures**	*FIFTH The Abstract was the VERY LAST section I wrote.* *The final touches. I did these while waiting for feedback from my supervisors on the Abstract.*
1 **Introduction** Incorporating and expanding on the original literature review: a full and updated review of existing literature, your rationale and the 'gap' which the thesis addresses, all of which leads to the aims and hypotheses.	*FOURTH The LAST chapter I wrote. You can only write a good intro once you have a good first draft of the rest and know (a) what your data show and (b) the structure of the thesis.*
2 **Methods 1** Review of the development of methods used to measure … (x)	*FIRST I wrote up the Methods chapters. 'What you did' is a statement of fact. This will never change but your memory of it will. So write it down as you go and before you forget. Detail everything so someone reading your thesis could replicate your study. Much of the fine detail may go in the Appendices.*
3 **Methods 2** Review of the development of methods to measure (y)	

4	**Experiment 1** Application of methods (from 2 and 3). Results, conclusions and further questions raised which lead to …	*SECOND I wrote up the experimental chapters. 'What you found' in each experiment will inform the design and direction of the next study – back to methods and repeat.*
5	**Experiment 2** Builds on the findings of Experiment 1. Results, conclusions and further questions raised which lead to …	
6	**Experiment 3** Builds on the findings of Experiments 1 and 2. Results and conclusions	
7	**Conclusions** Discussion of the findings from each experiment in relation to the others and in the light of existing knowledge. Implications for experimental practice (improvements) Implications for future research	*THIRD Then I wrote my conclusions chapter. 'What your findings mean' tells the story of where your research led. This is where you can demonstrate the relevance to the wider academic community and future directions for research.*
Appendices, Acknowledgements **Bibliography/references**		*I created Appendices and Acknowledgements as I went along.*

Thesis structure 4: PhD by publication

A PhD by publication consists of a number of journal articles (typically a minimum of four in peer-reviewed journals) and a 20,000–30,000-word critical analysis of the context for the publications. Check the exact requirements of your institution.

Some PhD students also include a wider range of works or pieces (e.g. CDs, field reports) that indicate the scope and application of their research. Articles should be arranged in intellectual order (not chronological order of publication), telling a coherent story of the evolution of the research and its contribution to the field. This is linked to the argument in the critical review.

First, the examiner wants to get an overview of your argument and of your skill as an author. Before reading the thesis from start to finish, they turn the pages …

- Preliminaries including abstract
- Introduction
- Conclusion: Is it consistent? Joined at the hip to the introduction?
- Methodology, to see your structure, your approach – where it came from and where it goes.
- References – to get an impression of the range and depth of your research. They will, of course, look to see if you have cited their work appropriately and accurately.

Then they are ready to read it from start to finish.

The preliminaries: first impressions

This section contains the following elements:

- Acknowledgements
- Abstract
- Contents list
- Lists of tables, figures

These will be the very last bits you write. As you look at other theses, you'll find out how important they are in forming an impression in your mind as a reader – so as a writer, don't rush it in an all-nighter!

I had put off writing the abstract as it always seemed so onerous, but when I was up against it I wrote it in 20 minutes ...

Acknowledgements

These offer an insight into you and how you worked: key influences on your thinking, your working relationships and a little bit of you ...

Thank everyone who helped and supported you, with an indication of how they contributed:

▶ your supervisory team by name
▶ others who advised or inspired you in some way – acknowledge any debt that is not reflected in your references
▶ participants/subjects (perhaps more generally)
▶ people who offered practical help
▶ friends and family.

And do make sure you show the bit of you that you *want* your readers to see!

The abstract

As an expert abstract reader in your day-to-day research, you know what you want to see in an abstract!

Try writing your abstract in these four short paragraphs.
1 **The research question**: why your research was needed – the gap in knowledge.
2 **How you did it**.
3 **What you found**: general findings and a brief mention of anything that stood out for you.
4 **Conclusions**: your takeaway points, and your contribution to knowledge.

The abstract (typically 200–300 words) is the single most important part of your thesis. It is your showcase – it will be the *only* contact between your work and the wider academic world on an electronic database, and eventually in the electronic Index to Theses (www.theses.com). You have a few moments to engage another researcher before they click to the next abstract. … So make yours count!

You want to convey a feeling of crisp, calm authority, written by a person (not a machine), that tells the story of your research. Read it aloud; ask others to read it. Above all, work on it, give it time.

The contents list

Your reader will want to get an overview of the structure and coherence of your thesis.

Make sure the Contents shows the logic of your organisation. Bald chapter headings may not be enough, but nor will your reader want to drown in detailed subheadings – make decisions about appropriateness.

Lists of tables, figures, illustrations, glossary

These give an indication of the detail of your work and your thoroughness as a researcher.

Make it easy to:
▶ navigate your thesis
▶ showcase the meticulousness of your compilation
▶ find and return to key material.

11 The introduction and conclusion

These two chapters are the key elements in the craft of constructing a thesis. The introduction is presented first but is written – or at least revised – last, when you know exactly what you are introducing. The conclusion is written after all the other chapters – most probably immediately before you write the introduction. In this way you know that your promise of what lies ahead (in the introduction) is indeed fulfilled (in the conclusion), and conversely, that the point you arrive at in the conclusion is indeed a logical progression from the introduction.

The introduction

The introduction locates your reader in the wider territory, surrounding field, particular area and specific problem of your research. You open the story of your research, how you approached it, why you did it that way. You will also give your reader an overview of the whole thesis, with a brief outline of each chapter – another opportunity to highlight your argument.

You may, however, be advised to write your introduction first, so it can act as a route map as you write. Supervisors often ask for an introduction at an early stage, possibly before you have a clear idea of where you will end up. This is a valid exercise in drafting, developing your argument, identifying where you have got to. You may well draw on these drafts in the final version, but an introduction written early in your research will not be the finished product.

You can think of your introduction as having two main movements.

An hourglass model for introductions

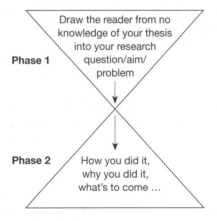

Phase 1 — Draw the reader from no knowledge of your thesis into your research question/aim/problem

Phase 2 — How you did it, why you did it, what's to come …

The first phase will be familiar to readers of *Planning Your PhD*: the five moves of an introduction to a research plan (pp. 100–4), justifying the aim. In some subjects, particularly science, this may be the preferred structure for the introduction to the completed PhD.

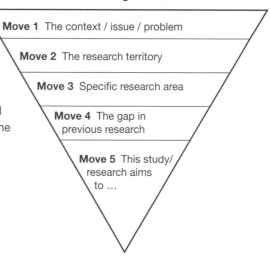

Phase 1: drawing the reader in …

Move 1 The context / issue / problem

Move 2 The research territory

Move 3 Specific research area

Move 4 The gap in previous research

Move 5 This study/ research aims to …

Phase 2: where next …?

In other disciplines, the introduction needs a second phase, to lead the reader to the research itself: how and why you carried it out, and what next?

How?
- Your methodology
- Key theorists
- Source materials
- Problems
- Limits of your study
- Definitions of key terms

Why?
- The 'story' of your research – show reflexivity by acknowledging your own position in the research
- Your contribution to literature/practice/policy (more fully articulated in your conclusion)

What's next?
- Thesis structure
- Preliminary hypotheses
- Hint at your overall argument (to whet the reader's appetite), but don't give it all away!

By the end of the introduction, your reader is engaged. You have opened the story of your research and now they are moving into it. Because you wrote it (or at least revised it) after you wrote your conclusion, the reader will be in for a good read …

The conclusion

In your conclusion you draw the strands of your research together, and immediately move on to consider the contribution your research has made, and where it might go next.

In the UK the research conclusions will be more carefully scrutinised in the future in the light of the requirements of the REF to demonstrate the impact of research on the wider community. It is worth reiterating, however, that the contribution to knowledge, to scholarship, is the route by which all research demonstrates its value.

Workshop 5: The elements of your conclusion

Consider which of these elements you will use to structure your conclusion:

1 Restatement of the problem you addressed
2 What you learnt – a summary chapter by chapter, drawing the strands together
3 Your contribution to knowledge – implications for scholarship, the literature
4 Implications for policy or practice (if appropriate)
5 The unanswered questions – implications for future research

Some of these elements will be more relevant to you than others: use these to develop your argument for the value of your research.

12 Become an editor!

There comes a point when you take off your writing hat, and become an editor …

- Do your sums. How many words do you have for each chapter? The introduction and conclusion will be a bit shorter. What is left to divide between the rest?
- Do you really need that quotation/example/cameo in your text or can you simply reference it?
- Does the chapter need a radical reshape? To be divided into two?

If you see your reader's eyes glazing over, perhaps it is more complicated than it needs to be …

- Check your tenses – do not write in the future tense. Especially check 'cut and pasted' material from previous drafts of your methodology. This is now 'what you did' – use the past tense.

- Be ruthless, but make sure nothing is lost! Cut and paste the deleted text into another document and save it as 'Cuts to x version y'.
- Date all files and keep copies of earlier drafts until your final write-up.
- If you can remove a word from a sentence without changing the meaning, take it out.

And, crucially, have you cited your external examiner's work? They will go straight to your bibliography/references to see whether your citation is relevant and accurate – it may act as a proxy for your thoroughness throughout.

Try and make your thesis a good read, one in which your voice shines through. Introduce, recap and conclude points throughout your sections and chapters. You may be able to do this directly:

> In this thesis I examine the … After introducing (…) I … In this chapter I review three sets of literature concerning … I now turn to a second theoretical concern … In this concluding chapter I …

If 'I' as a written style is not encouraged in your discipline/institution/department, you will be developing a written style of your own that can perform the same function. Guide your reader through your thesis, introducing and concluding each chapter and section. If you do this throughout, you will create a pattern of expectation in your reader – which will help your argument become more familiar and be easier to follow.

As you reach the final stages of your PhD, you will need to answer some important questions:

▶ Will I be able to complete a final draft by the deadline agreed with my supervisors?

▶ If so, will this draft be good enough to submit for examination?

▶ If not, can I extend my deadline?

▶ And if I do this, what will the impact be on my funding/finances/career plans/ life plans'?

Your supervisors can advise you on whether your latest drafts are at or near the level required for submission. Take this advice seriously. The standards that you set yourself may either exceed or fall short of those demanded by PhD examiners, and so your own feelings of needing more time, or wanting to finish, may not be the most accurate indicator of whether you are ready to submit. If you submit your thesis against your supervisor's advice, you risk failure and wasting years of work. Conversely, if your supervisor recommends that you submit, but you wish to continue, it may help to consider:

▶ your PhD thesis as an examination document, not the definitive work on the subject

- that submission does not have to be the end of your research, just the end of your PhD. Further lines of inquiry can be followed up in your postdoctoral research
- the value of the changes you want to make to your thesis, versus the benefits of completion for your finances/career/life.

If you and your supervisors decide that your chances of success would be improved by prolonging your PhD, various options may be open to you depending on your university and method of funding (some grants and bursaries have very strict rules regarding completion). You may have the option to change to a different mode of study (e.g. part time or continuing status) and/or apply for an extension to your maximum period of registration. You will probably be required to justify these requests and provide a realistic timetable of your plans for completion.

When the end of your PhD is in sight, regular self-evaluations of your progress will help keep you focused on the finish line. Ask yourself:
- Has improving the thesis become tinkering?
- Have I stopped aiming at adequacy for the task and started aiming for perfection?
- Have I stopped thinking of my thesis as an exam-orientated document and started treating it as a masterwork?

If the answer to any of these questions is 'yes', then it is time to take yourself in hand and submit the thesis.

Checklist to help in preparing for submission

Do the following:

- Submit your final draft to your supervisors for scrutiny.
- Check your university's submission guidelines (how many copies? formatting requirements? binding requirements?).
- Complete the front and back matter of the thesis in accordance with your university's guidelines (e.g. title page, acknowledgements, contents page, bibliography).
- Arrange the printing of your thesis. If you need to submit a large number of copies you may want to consider using your university printing service or a commercial print shop. Even good desktop printers may struggle with a document the size of a thesis. You will need to leave sufficient time (possibly several days) if you choose to pay to get your thesis printed.
- Arrange to get your thesis soft bound at your university printing service or a commercial print shop. Large theses may need to be soft bound in several volumes.
- Call your university research office to arrange when and where to submit the thesis.

Then take a deep breath … and submit it!

What next?

After submitting your thesis ... slow down

You've been working intensively for months, and in the final weeks have been going full tilt to get all the final corrections done, with the stress of printing, binding etc. – and now it's in!

Then what? There is this sudden lull, a gap in your life. Give yourself time to recover and gather the mental energy to prepare for the final push to the viva. Take a break. ... Do something you haven't done for a long time ... give yourself a few treats. Start talking to friends and family again. Have fun, sleep well and ... **rejoin the human race!**

TALKING AND PRESENTING

Talking about your research is as important in developing your ideas as the writing that preoccupies PhD students. Any conversation can provide a 'Eureka!' moment when an idea clicks into place or you hear yourself argue from a new perspective. Talking helps you become more articulate and eloquent in expressing your thoughts in any presentation you do, and is an essential skill in defending your thesis in your viva.

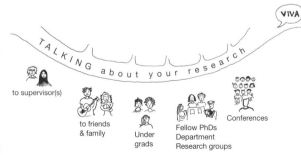

This section considers some of the ways in which you talk about your research, from informal chats to showcasing your work to 'expert' audiences at academic conferences.

14 Talking about your research

With family and friends

Explaining your research to non-experts – to family and friends and people you encounter day to day – is hard. You have to find a way to describe difficult concepts in plain language. This helps to crystallise your thoughts and strip away the jargon to get back to the essence of your research questions and your findings. Get talking – it keeps you in touch with people!

With supervisors

Throughout your PhD, you will meet with your supervisor(s) on a regular basis.

Supervisors may see their role as:

▶ the critic, wanting to see each chapter, reading, discussing and suggesting revisions

▶ the coach, who wants to talk with their supervisee throughout, and is more interested in their pathway and logic.

Both styles of supervision engage students in discussion, and require you to articulate your ideas and justify your argument: you will talk, you will argue and sometimes you might convince your supervisor of your idea. Equally there will be times when your discussions reveal that you need to drop a particular thread, or that the method you believed to be foolproof is not working.

These are privileged occasions, and it is hardly surprising that more frequent meetings appear to contribute to PhD students' success (Seagram et al. 1998; Sinclair 2004). So make best use of meetings with your supervisor(s), and prepare carefully: identify a particular aim or goal, list of questions, or a data set to discuss.

With PhD students

Discussing your work with PhD students from other disciplines will help you to present your ideas in a clear and academic way. PhD peers will critique in a way that is different from your supervisors or friends. Their perspectives can be immensely helpful: *But could that argument be taken another way … ?* or *In my discipline, we would take a more structured approach; have you tried x?*

With academic staff

The question 'So how is the PhD going?' keeps you talking about the how, the what and the why. Many staff in the university will have done PhDs themselves, and can offer a sympathetic ear – if you can keep talking about your work, you will keep developing it.

At departmental presentations

Presenting your work at a departmental seminar or research group meeting may appear to be a distraction from the primary business of writing, but it is in fact an opportunity to:

- fine-tune your argument by articulating why you are there, what you hope to do with your PhD, and what you have found so far
- present your work to many intelligent and interested colleagues in one go
- get feedback on a talk you plan to present at a conference, or an article you plan to write
- gain helpful suggestions for improvements, or to flag up relevant topics colleagues think may interest you.

Your department may, however, represent a narrow field of views ...

15 Conferences

The true test of your argument will happen when you take it to audiences beyond the safety of your university. Conferences are an essential step to becoming a well-rounded academic, and provide vital networking opportunities, so select your conferences carefully.

How to afford that conference!

Bear in mind the following:

- Singapore sounds glamorous, but there may be an equally prestigious (and perhaps more relevant) conference down the road.
- Look out for student concessions and attendance bursaries (offered by some organisations which host annual conferences).
- Take advantage of early-bird registration fee rates.
- Present a paper or poster – you are more likely to receive funding assistance if you do.
- Book travel and accommodation in advance – it may be cheaper.

Presenting your work

You can present your work at a conference in a number of ways:

▶ an individual paper or presentation: you write a paper/prepare the presentation and present it
▶ a group presentation: you present research you have worked on with one or more colleague(s) and present it together
▶ a poster presentation (sometimes linked with a workshop).

Responding to a call for papers

When you respond to a call for papers, you will usually **submit an abstract** providing a summary of your talk.

Seek advice from your supervisor about submitting an abstract. They will be able to offer useful perspectives on matters like:

▶ collaborating in writing the paper – useful to develop your academic credentials
▶ writing your abstract in order to maximise the chances of its acceptance
▶ deciding how much of the story you want to tell in your abstract (you want delegates to be intrigued enough to attend your presentation but you do not want to jeopardise future publication by having your results published in a conference abstract)

- checking the rules for submitting an article for publication with your target journals (see their 'Instructions to authors'), to ensure that there is no potential conflict of interest with your plan to submit a conference abstract.

If you do decide to submit an abstract make sure you follow the instructions about the format and structure meticulously (check the conference website for details). Allow plenty of time before the deadline: the quality of your abstract will influence not only your chances of acceptance but also the decisions of participants on whether to attend your talk.

If your abstract is accepted, you have plenty of time to prepare as the conference date is likely to be many months away. Use the time to practise your talk to as many audiences as possible, and work out how best to control the nerves! Employ techniques such as prompt cards, practising your technology, timing yourself, breathing deeply …

For the day itself, can you find a colleague who will be a friendly face in the audience for you to focus on, look interested and nod or ask you specific questions?

Fifteen to 20 minutes is the usual time given to present your work, and then the Chair of the session will ask the audience for questions. This is the most nerve-wracking aspect of conference presentations. Yet, it is also potentially the most valuable: you get new insights into your work and it is good practice both for defending your ideas and for taking advice from others.

The purpose of conferences is to share ideas and promote research, so people may well criticise your research question, method and theories, but then offer some supportive advice on how you might progress further.

Responses to questions

Think about these openers for difficult questions:

'That is a good question, and something we have been thinking about …'

'Thank you, I was hoping someone would pick up on that, and that is a question we want to look at next …'

'I don't know, do you have any thoughts on that?' (There is nothing wrong in admitting you don't know the answer if you don't!)

'I would need to think about the answer to that; perhaps we could have a chat later.'

It is unlikely but possible that someone in the audience may fire difficult questions at you, though it is not usual to do this to a PhD student. You need, however, to be prepared to argue your corner. A student who can give a well-thought-out answer to a tricky question on the spot will impress colleagues, supervisors and (in a conference setting) maybe even your future viva examiner(s) or employer.

Friends, family, supervisor and a colleague – I got them all to fire questions at me. I don't like speaking off the cuff …

BUT

If you do get a hypercritical questioner, do not get defensive. Watch how other people respond to criticism. Take a deep breath and consider the following:

▸ **Is the criticism valid?** Maybe you need to explain a point more clearly, or maybe there are improvements you can make for future studies.

> *I was 'grilled' by a very eminent professor in a question session, ... Later she came up and explained that she was not devaluing what I was doing – she thought it was good – she was just getting me to look at it from a different perspective.*

▸ **How can you refute what they say?** They may be wrong – but you need to demonstrate why in your answer: maybe they have misunderstood a point, and you therefore need to provide clarification.

▸ **How can you defend your research?** You have the right to defend it, but avoid being defensive or making statements you cannot back up with evidence.

▸ **It is not a trial**, and if you feel someone is being downright rude, just smile and thank them for their contribution.

An alternative to presenting a paper is to give a poster presentation. Sometimes you may be invited to give a short presentation based on your poster.

There is usually a dedicated time for poster viewings. If you are lucky and the poster display is near the refreshments area, lots of people will browse the posters. Your poster needs to grab the attention of passing delegates and convey your message quickly and succinctly – you can then talk to people about your work.

Preparing a poster display

Your audience will decide within a few seconds whether they want to continue reading your poster. You have only a limited time to engage them in deeper conversation. So … prepare carefully.

Who is your audience?

Who will be at the conference? Are there particular people you want to make contact with? What key words would attract them to your poster?

What's your message?

What is the one message you want to convey to someone in just 3 seconds? Will you convey it in the title, an image or diagram?

Design to meet conference requirements

Follow the organisers' specifications for poster size (e.g. A1, A0) and orientation (landscape or portrait); and bring your own fixings anyway.

Design for maximum impact

That message you want to convey needs to jump out at a reader from a distance of 3 metres – you want to pull your readers in from across the room.

▶ For the title use few words and a bold font (about 90 point)
▶ The rest of the text on the poster needs to be big enough to read at a distance of 1 metre (about 30 pt).

Get help! There is lots of helpful advice on the web to start you thinking:

- Try to provide a clear entry point for readers, and a logical visual flow.
- Group related information.
- Use numbering or arrows if linked content should be read in a particular order.
- Avoid either oversimplifying (too little useful information) or overcomplicating (too much information).
- Use blank space and margins to give your content room to breathe.

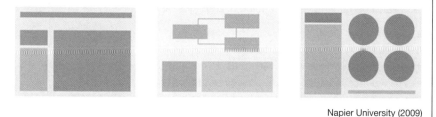

Napier University (2009)

Check what help your university can offer: poster templates, printing and laminating? Of course you can always phone a friend (especially one with a talent for design ...).

Create opportunities for follow-up

Prepare a one-page flier summarising the poster so that people can read about your research in their own time. Ensure your name and contact details are clearly displayed: firstly, to establish research ownership and, secondly, to provide a channel for future communication. If possible, have a supply of contact cards too.

And finally: arrive early to mount your poster display to best effect – and perhaps to have a choice of display space.

We all talked our ways through our PhDs: we talked to develop and consolidate ideas, to exchange ideas and engage in lively dialogue with colleagues, to convey our ideas to work colleagues, and to convey our ideas to a wider audience at conferences and workshops around the globe. For all of us this talking was essential practice for the most important discussion we would face during our PhDs: the viva voce …

THE ORAL EXAMINATION: THE VIVA

In those countries that use the viva, it is the second strand of the examination to assess whether you have reached the standard of 'Doctorateness' in the process and presentation of

'Viva voce' – Latin for 'the live voice' – an oral examination

your research. It is an invitation to you to defend your work in response to probing questions by experts in the field, your examiners. The viva, also known as an 'oral defence', allows you to demonstrate your understanding in a different way from the written form of your thesis. Talking and writing are different forms of assessment, and each is valid in its own right.

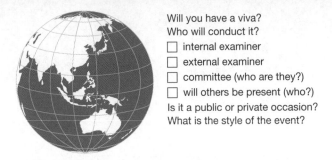

Will you have a viva?
Who will conduct it?
- [ ] internal examiner
- [ ] external examiner
- [ ] committee (who are they?)
- [ ] will others be present (who?)

Is it a public or private occasion?
What is the style of the event?

This section offers practical advice about anticipating the questions you will be asked, about how to prepare, how to perform and what comes after … and offers you a window on an experience largely hidden from view.

Enjoy the satisfaction that comes with submitting your thesis. It is done and you can tinker no longer! So, once you have relaxed a little, it is time to start looking ahead at the final hurdle to becoming a 'Doctor'.

18 The examiner and the examiners' report

Whether held in public or private, the viva will follow a pattern. It is the examiners' job to encourage you to demonstrate and defend your work, ideas and thesis.

The examiner

In essence the examiner will want you to explain:

▶ the *point*: why you did it
▶ the *value* of what you achieved.

An examiner explains this more fully:

- I want to be reassured that the candidate knows their literature, that they did the work themselves, and understand it. I ask them to explain their ideas, their choices of method and how they theorised to develop the work.
- I want to know how it was for the candidate. Have they enjoyed the work? What aspects were challenging, frustrating, rewarding? Do they understand the limitations of their work? If they could do it again, what might they do differently?
- I view it as the candidate's rare opportunity to 'shine': to be the centre of attention. I plan questions to facilitate talk because I want them to demonstrate their expert knowledge and contribution to the subject area.
- I point out any shortcomings of the thesis and provide opportunities for the candidate to discuss them and offer solutions.

(Mary Richardson, co-author)

The examiner's 'Final Report' checklist

The 'oral examination' is the second and final part of the PhD examination process. The examiners have already read and reported on the thesis (see Part 3). The 'Final Report' is based on the additional insights the candidate shows face to face.

Typically an examiner's viva checklist will look something like this:

	The type of questions the examiner will consider
1	Are you satisfied that the thesis presented is the candidate's own work?
2	Did the candidate show a satisfactory knowledge and understanding of background studies and matters relating to the thesis?
3	In the case of a candidate whose research programme is part of a collaborative project, did the oral examination demonstrate that the candidate's own contribution what worthy of the award?
4	Other comments on the oral examination.

Reproduced (with minor alterations) with thanks to Oxford Brookes University Research degrees subcommittee (2010).

You will notice how these questions complement the checklist for the 'Preliminary' report completed by the examiners (p. 43) on reading the thesis. The difference here is that you will be answering them live, where there is no hiding place. The great benefit/ advantage of this is that you can pursue the defence of your thesis, address examiners' questions directly, showcase your mastery of your subject, and draw on all your skills as a communicator ...

19 Preparing for the viva

Find out when your viva will be. Typically it will be 2 to 3 months after submission of your thesis, but it is alarmingly dependent on the circumstances of the individual examiner – illness can delay it, or a change in travel arrangements can bring it forward (to 3 weeks after submission, in one case we know of!). Administrative delays on the part of your university can delay it up to 6 months. It is a moveable feast.

After submission (and a few days' rest)

Put the thesis to one side, step back, reflect on your PhD as a whole, and …

Read Continue to read around your subject area, especially recent journal articles, and particularly those of your examiners. Being able to discuss research that has appeared since you submitted your thesis will show that you really have kept up to date.

Talk Use the feeling of success on submission of your thesis to boost your confidence in talking about your research: present papers at conferences, departmental seminars, workshops, discussion groups. Offer to give specialist lectures (on both undergraduate and Master's programmes) in your department.

Engage Continue to participate in any supportive PhD forums, or departmental social events you normally take part in. Don't let yourself become isolated at this time.

Gather information Now is the time to find out about what to expect at your viva and deal with the logistical issues. Your supervisor and recent PhD students will be your most valuable sources of information. Most universities will have online or video resources about the viva. Find out:

- **where** and **when** the viva will take place. Ask to see the room and even where you will be seated if this will help you. You may have some flexibility in choice of day and time depending on both your and your examiners' availability.
- **how long** vivas typically last in your field: 1 to 3 hours is the norm. Your institution may suggest the length of a viva in instructions to examiners.
- **who** will be present. What are the roles of those present? Can your supervisor take notes?
- **what** additional materials you can take in with you. An annotated copy of your thesis is essential.

Do you have someone who can come and meet/celebrate/comfort/collect you afterwards?

Revisit Look back through your diary or journal entries charting your research journey, to remind yourself of conference and seminar presentations and papers submitted.

Keep yourself fit, healthy and rested You need to cope physically and mentally with robust and possibly lengthy questioning at the viva.

Finally, double-check your thesis

- Spelling and typos
- Bibliography: are references correct and consistent (especially those of your examiners)?
- Tense: is your writing consistently in either the present or the past tense? Your methodology should be in the past tense.

'Typos are inexcusable,' said one experienced examiner.

It is worth marking all errors in the copy of your thesis which you will take into the viva with you. This degree of preparation will impress the examiners and also alert you to possible queries the examiners may raise.

In the final run-up

In the 2 or 3 weeks before your viva, re-immerse yourself in the thesis. Prepare in a strategic way, as follows.

By then I had developed a love/hate relationship with my thesis. I needed a complete break from it and concentrated all my preparation into one week ...

Plan your time

Arrange a date for a mock viva with your supervisory team about a week before the viva. Questions in mock vivas may be very different from those that come up in the real viva, but the process of dealing with unforeseen questions and speaking aloud to academics is still valuable.

My mock viva was useful ... because I realised I had got into the habit of simplifying ideas for my students rather than articulating them in their full complexity ...

Revise strategically

Consider which of these might work for you:

- Label each chapter with a coloured tag so that you can quickly and effortlessly flip between chapters.
- Break down your revision into identified themes. The obvious division is by thesis chapter.
- Re-read each chapter and the *main* references. Don't sweat the small stuff! Knowing the key literature well is more important than remembering the details of every single paper you have referenced.
- Summarise each chapter in a few points (on Post-it® notes or cards to take in with you). Note the key points you want to cover: your research question; your distinct contribution to knowledge; your key findings; your methods.

- If you conducted empirical research, re-run analyses to remind yourself of how and why you treated and analysed your data the way you did. It will also remind you of the methodological limitations you faced, and the additional studies you would have liked to run if you had more time.
- Prepare and rehearse a 2-minute summary of what your thesis is about: what you did, why you did it, what you found. This is often the first question examiners ask.
- Scan recent literature in your area and add Post-its® at the relevant points in the thesis to remind you of this latest research (especially that which relates to your examiners' work).

And finally

Write a list of potential questions, based on:
- the typical pattern of questions (see p. 43)
- advice from your supervisory team
- talking to other PhD students
- your research into your examiners' approaches, preferences and track records: writing style, theoretical stance and preferred methodology. Are you in general agreement or do you have different approaches? What are their criticisms likely to be, and how strong might they be?

On the day

▸ Wear smart and comfortable clothes with layers you can add or take off.

▸ Arrive in good time.

▸ Enjoy the sense of anticipation! Adrenalin will help to sharpen you up!

*When I arrived the place was deserted –
it turned out they were all still at lunch ...*

Prepare yourself mentally

Visualise yourself in the viva talking calmly, answering questions and engaging in an interesting discussion with your examiner. Remind yourself that you know more about your research than anyone else and your examiners are interested in hearing about it.

Go into your viva with a positive attitude and an understanding that you will be tested in a fair and well-regulated manner. Codes of practice for viva examiners and candidates have become better regulated over the years (QAA 2004). The presence of the Chair, and at least one internal examiner (and a public audience in some countries), will ensure that your viva is witnessed by several independent parties.

Ask your supervisor(s) to make a note of proceedings: questions asked and how you answered, suggestions by the examiner(s) in case you have to make corrections – such as additional analyses of data, alternative interpretations of the results and so forth. Examiners may also make suggestions for publication.

The performance

The main performers are you and your examiner(s). Answer directly to the person asking the question and give balanced attention to all examiners throughout. Ignore your supervisors and everyone else unless they are actively addressing you (for example, the Chair may suggest a short break if it is a long viva). For this performance you and your examiners are the key players.

The moves of the viva

Vivas tend to follow a format, so there are phases you can anticipate …

1 What's it about?

The examiners start by asking you to give a statement as to what your thesis is *about*. You talk for 10–15 minutes. You're on terra firma; relax, get into it.

They started by saying how much they had enjoyed my thesis … Then it changed …

Clarify for the examiner the crucial points of your thesis:

▶ *why* did you carry out the research? The purpose …
▶ your principal arguments
▶ your principal findings.

2 What is your methodology?

'Tell us about the strengths and weaknesses of your methodology. Why did you design it that way? Why isn't it <u>better</u> …?'

This is about defining the limits of your enterprise – what it does and does not do.

The examiner will be getting picky here – picking holes in your work, giving every appearance of getting annoyed with you.

I had been warned that it would feel as if the examiners were really getting pissed off with me ...

They openly expressed their dissatisfaction with my answers ... they told me they were not convinced by my argument and aspects of my methodology.

Keep cool. This is an opportunity to show your own critical awareness of the strengths and weaknesses of your methodology.

The younger one threw tough question after tough question ... 'Mixed methods ... well I'm not a fan of them ...'

The best survival tactic, I think, is to treat the viva as a game in which your challenge is to maintain your composure ...

3 What is the bigger picture?

In a wider sense:

- What are the implications of your research?
- For scholarship? What does it add to what is already established?
- For practice? For policy?
- If you were going on to do further research, what is important? What areas might you pursue?

When I was called back they said they thought my thesis was excellent ...

Embrace criticism of your work and keep an open mind. Your examiners are experts too and they may have ideas to contribute that will elevate your work further; accept ideas and suggestions with good grace. You can give ground without undermining your own thesis: *'That criticism has merit, but I didn't do it that way because ...'*

Give full answers and pause to consider exactly what the examiner is asking you. Explain the point, why you did it, its value. If you feel you have suddenly stopped, ask 'Does that answer your question?' and the examiners may offer you additional prompts.

However, it is up to you to give full answers, not short answers. Examiners don't want to have to scratch around thinking up additional questions or prompts to extract an answer from a PhD candidate. The purpose of the viva is to allow you to take the floor: a question is an invitation to expand, not to answer in a bullet point.

Make full use of your annotated thesis. It is often useful to take a moment to turn to a relevant page in the thesis to help you answer a question (for example to refer the examiner to a graph, diagram, illustration, or maybe to remind yourself of a forgotten name or fact).

Honesty is the best policy. Never try to bluff – if you do not know the answer to a question, say so and move on.

Where it is appropriate, especially in a PhD by publication, discuss the work you have published and open a dialogue about where you might publish in the future.

Reflections: the ritual nature of the viva

The viva voce examination has a long history, and its enactment is governed by certain rituals, although these vary greatly among the countries that have adopted it. These ritual aspects give the viva a 'weight' and importance that may feel overwhelming (Crossouard 2011 p21), but can also be reassuring. Like all rituals, vivas have certain rules of performance that, if followed, function to transform the participant from one status to another. You, your examiners, your supervisors and any others who are present at your viva have particular roles to play for the duration of the ritual. The role of your examiners is to question you, sometimes robustly, on the process and outcomes of your research.

Don't be surprised if the persona they adopt is more critical than in your previous encounters with them – this is part of the performance. Your role is the calm, confident candidate who is well prepared and unflustered by the questions. You've had 'walk-on parts' in the past at conferences and seminars; the mock viva is your dress rehearsal, and the viva is your big performance. You need to rehearse (talk out loud and record and play back your answers), learn the script (your key statements and answers) and engage in some method acting to help you begin to assume the role of 'doctor'.

Once the viva ends you will usually be asked to wait outside whilst the examiners make their decision. In truth, they have often made it before you walk in the door, but nevertheless a poor viva might result in an outcome that means more work for you. When you are called back, you will learn the outcome. With some variation between countries, typically these are:

▶ Pass – no corrections.

▶ Pass – minor corrections. These can include: typos, addition or deletion of a small amount of text; some other amendments requested by the examiners – normally to be completed within about 4 weeks.

> *I passed subject to minor corrections. As they were listed I became quite angry – they were so minor. One paragraph and a lot of fiddling with pagination ...*

▶ Pass – major amendments and corrections. This usually means some more substantive work, e.g. revising of a section or several chapters of the text – to be completed typically within 6 months.

▶ Award of an MPhil – the examiners did not feel the work was of doctoral standard, but did feel it merited a Master's qualification (possibly with additional time).

▶ Resubmission and re-examination – of thesis, viva or both within a time frame.

▶ Fail – the work failed, without the option of resubmission.

The last three options are very unusual indeed. Your supervisory team will have advised you to submit, so you are only likely to fail if you chose to submit your thesis against the advice of your supervisors. So this is not something to worry about ...

And afterwards ...

Your viva is a stressful day; you have prepared, you have been doing this work for years and it is very important to you. How you will feel after the event is difficult to predict. It is natural to feel disappointed or upset if you don't get the outcome you were hoping for, but it is also common to find your response to a PhD success is more muted than you expected.

If you passed with corrections then it is best to deal with these as soon as possible. Examiners will need time to read the corrections and give feedback to you on whether you have addressed their concerns sufficiently for them to pass the thesis. Once the examiners are happy that all corrections have been made, you may get hardbound copies of the thesis made and submitted to the University according to your institution's guidelines.

LIFE AFTER YOUR PHD

If your viva is successful, it marks the end of one phase of your life and the beginning of another. Your focus on completion, and then the viva, may have made it difficult to visualise life after the PhD, and when it arrives it can feel disorientating.

This section is intended to help you give shape and purpose to your new post-PhD world.

One hour later …

You will still be tingling from the thrill of being told that you have (or soon will have) passed your PhD, the shiny, new sound of 'Doctor' before your name reverberating in your head. Phone calls to your nervous family members and friends are a good opportunity to bask in your well-deserved glory. Depending on your relationships with your supervisors and examiners, they may want to celebrate with you too.

But before you let your examiners escape, don't forget to garner their advice on the post-PhD prospects for your thesis. Do they think your PhD is suitable for publication? As a book, journal articles, or both? Which sections of the work would convert particularly well into articles and book chapters? And which journals would be most suitable for your work? After you have plumbed the depths of their expertise, sit back, relax and celebrate. You deserve it.

Over the next few days ...

These early days, before you get too involved in your next project, are a good opportunity to start introducing your thesis to the world beyond your supervisory team. Find out from your university what their regulations and recommendations are for getting your thesis hardbound. Your university will probably want at least one hardbound copy for its university library (and your graduation may be conditional on supplying this), but you may want to get extra copies bound for:

) you to display in a prominent place on your most visible bookshelf
) any close family or friends who you want to thank for their support
) your supervisors, if they request it.

This type of binding can be rather expensive, however, so you may want to avoid giving a copy to everyone you have ever met.

Ask your university about submitting your thesis to EThOS, the British Library's Electronic Theses Online System (this is replacing the British Library Thesis Service). You will need to complete a Deposit Agreement giving details of the thesis, including keywords for search purposes. Consider carefully who you would like to read your thesis (policy makers, researchers in particular disciplines, students) and what keywords they may search for. Your university may also have its own online repository for theses which can give your thesis international exposure.

One week later ...

The afterglow of viva success is beginning to fade, and it might be time to start thinking about the future. It is an unfortunate truth that a PhD does not necessarily guarantee you a job, or a promotion. What it does provide you with, however, are the skills with which to build and disseminate a research profile around your PhD that will get you noticed.

These are precisely the skills we have focused upon in this book: **talking** and **writing**. You can use these skills to:

- re**write** your CV, drawing attention to your doctorate and the skills you have gained from it
- begin to **write** applications for jobs or postdoctoral research posts that require a PhD
- offer to give a **talk** on your research at universities or organisations that you would like to work at
- give papers at relevant conferences and use the opportunity to **talk** to others in your field about your research and any possible vacancies.

These activities will help you to begin to reorientate your research towards purposes beyond the PhD.

One month later ...

If you wish to have an academic career, a PhD may not be enough to get a job – you also need to have publications, and, since academic posts normally include a teaching load, some teaching experience.

Now is a good time to gain experience of various forms of teaching, and if this is not possible, look into giving invited lectures to undergraduate and Master's students at your institution.

If you have not begun to publish during your PhD, you might want to consider the following:

▶ Journal articles are quicker to publish than books. They allow you to stake your claim to your research area without waiting for book publication, which can take several years.
▶ Writing a journal article is not the same as writing a PhD chapter. Sections of your thesis may be suitable for conversion into journal articles if they:
  ▶ are at the leading edge of research in your discipline
  ▶ make a single, clear argument
  ▶ are the right length for submissions to the journal you have selected.

▶ Give yourself some time and distance from the thesis-writing process (some publishers recommend a year) before attempting to convert your thesis into

That summer felt really strange. For the first time in 6 years there wasn't something I 'ought' to be writing. Now, with a bit of distance, I'm starting to work on journal articles ...

a book (if this is encouraged in your discipline). A PhD is an examination document and you will need to make a number of changes to make it into a commercially viable publication. The more time that has elapsed since the end of your PhD, the more clearly you will be able to recognise these differences and implement the necessary alterations. You may also discover new angles on your research that will make the reworking process more creative and enjoyable.

In the next year ...

You will be invited to graduate. This is a wonderful way to bring closure to years of hard graft, and

I guess I've metamorphosed into a different creature as a result of doing the PhD ...

to celebrate with those who have supported you. You will have the opportunity to wear the silliest of all academic hats, and to participate in a ceremony of academic pomp that reminds you that you have achieved something special. Enjoy it!

References

Booth W, Columb G and Williams J (1995). *The craft of research*. Chicago: University of Chicago Press.

Crossouard B (2011). The doctoral viva voce as a cultural practice: the gendered production of academic subjects. *Gender and Education*. (forthcoming).

Higher Education Funding Council for England (2007). PhD research degrees: update. Available at www.hefce.ac.uk/pubs/hefce/2007/07_28/ [Accessed 26 January 2011]

Napier University (2009). Academic posters. Available at www2.napier.ac.uk/getready/writing_presenting/academic_posters.html#impact [Accessed 26 January 2011]

Orwell G (1946). Politics and the English language. *The collected essays, journalism and letters of George Orwell. Vol. 4: In front of your nose 1945–1950*. Harmondsworth: Penguin Books, p156–70.

Quality Assurance Agency (2004). Code of practice for the assurance of academic quality and standards in higher education. Section 1: Postgraduate research programmes. Available at www.qaa.ac.uk/academicinfrastructure/codeOfPractice/section1/default.asp [Accessed 26 January 2011]

Seagram B, Gould J and Pyke S (1998). An investigation of gender and other variables on time to completion of doctoral degrees. *Research in Higher Education*. 39(3) p28–31.

Simpson MJ (2003). *Hitchhiker: a biography of Douglas Adams*. Boston US: Justin, Charles and Co.

Sinclair M (2004). The pedagogy of 'good' PhD supervision: a national cross-disciplinary investigation of PhD supervision. Available at www.dest.gov.au/NR/rdonlyres/07C6492B-F1BE-45C6-A283-6098B6952D29/2536/phd_supervision.pdf [Accessed 26 January 2011]

University of Manchester (2010). *Academic phrasebank*. Available at www.phrasebank.manchester.ac.uk/sources.htm [Accessed 26 January 2011]

Useful sources

Trafford V and Leshem S (2008). *Stepping stones to achieving your doctorate.*
Maidenhead: Open University Press/McGraw-Hill Education.
Provides lists of general questions that are typically asked in vivas; your supervisors can provide a more subject-specific list. A thought-provoking book for thinking about the whole PhD from start to finish.

Wellington J (2010). Supporting students' preparation for the viva: their pre-conceptions and implications for practice. *Teaching in Higher Education.* 15(1) p71–84.
Provides an insightful list of questions students typically ask when planning for their viva (which focus on rules and regulations, appointment of examiners and conduct).

Index

ALSO IN THE POCKET STUDY SKILLS SERIES

POCKET STUDY SKILLS

Janet Godwin

PLANNING YOUR ESSAY

READING AND MAKING NOTES

POCKET STUDY SKILLS

Jeanne Godfrey

GETTING
CRITICAL

REFERENCING & UNDERSTANDING PLAGIARISM

POCKET STUDY SKILLS

Kate Williams & Jude Carroll

POCKET STUDY SKILLS
Julia Copus

BRILLIANT WRITING TIPS FOR STUDENTS